DOMINOES

The Jungle Book

Rudyard Kipling

T0355146

Series Editor: Nicole Irving

Founder Editors: Bill Bowler and Sue Parminter

Text adaptation by Alex Raynham

Illustrated by Stella Koh

Joseph Rudyard Kipling (1865–1936) was a British author of poetry and fiction. Born in Bombay, India, Kipling spent the first six years of his life there. He also went back to India to work when he was older. Kipling worked as a journalist, poet, novelist, and short story writer. He wrote *The Jungle Book* in 1894 as a collection of stories. Kipling won the Nobel Prize in Literature in 1907.

OXFORD
UNIVERSITY PRESS

OXFORD
UNIVERSITY PRESS

Great Clarendon Street, Oxford, OX2 6DP, United Kingdom

Oxford University Press is a department of the University of Oxford.
It furthers the University's objective of excellence in research, scholarship,
and education by publishing worldwide. Oxford is a registered trade
mark of Oxford University Press in the UK and in certain other countries

ISBN: 978 0 19 462720 7

Printed in China

This book is printed on paper from certified and well-managed sources

ACKNOWLEDGEMENTS

Illustrations and cover artwork by: Stella Koh/Astound US Inc

*The publisher would like to thank the following for their kind permission to use photographs
and other copyright material:* 123RF pp.25 (tiger fur/Anan Kaewkhammul), 42 (python/
Berangere Duforets), 44 (tiger/ewastudio), 44 (panther/Anton Ivanov), 44 (bear/lightpoet),
46 (red kites/Andrew Mark Astbury); Oxford University Press pp.24 (water buffalo/Jorg
Hackemann), 43 (elephant/neijia); Shutterstock pp.24 (Ladakh village/Taras Shchetinin),
25 (trail/Stefan Holm), 25 (hut/Matyas Rehak), 25 (fields/dennnis), 44 (wolf/Michael
Schroeder), 46 (Indian children/Alexandra Lande), 46 (Siberian tiger/Sergey Uryadnikov),
46 (wolves/Martin Prochazkacz), 46 (snakes/SvedOliver), 46 (deer/Juan de Santiago).

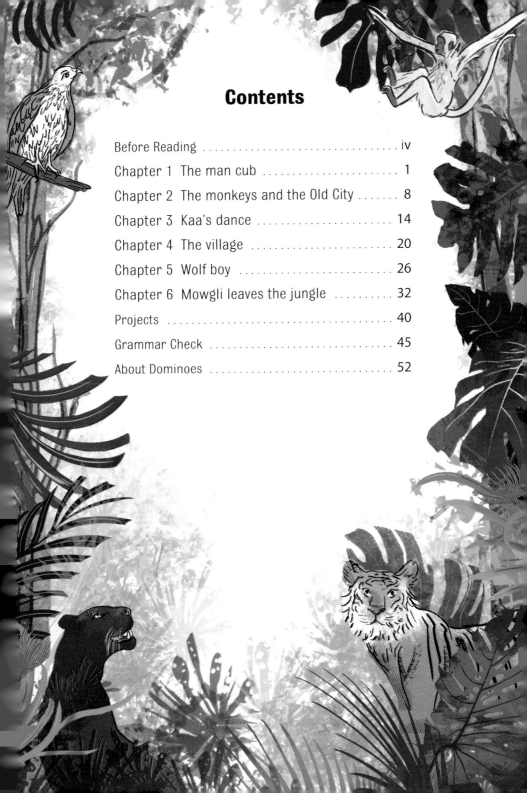

Contents

Before Reading iv

Chapter 1 The man cub 1

Chapter 2 The monkeys and the Old City 8

Chapter 3 Kaa's dance 14

Chapter 4 The village 20

Chapter 5 Wolf boy 26

Chapter 6 Mowgli leaves the jungle 32

Projects 40

Grammar Check 45

About Dominoes 52

BEFORE READING

1 Here are some characters from *The Jungle Book*. Match them with the animals in the box. Use a dictionary to help you.

bear   kite   panther   snake   tiger   ~~wolf~~

Akela	Shere Khan	Baloo

a ..... wolf .....   **b** ....   **c** ....

Bagheera	Chil	Kaa

d ....   **e** ....   **f** ....

2 In *The Jungle Book*, a boy called Mowgli lives in the jungle. What happens in the story? Tick (✔) four things.

- **a** Mowgli lives with a family of wolves. ☐
- **b** Shere Khan becomes his friend. ☐
- **c** Mowgli makes a house in the trees. ☐
- **d** Baloo and Bagheera teach Mowgli many things. ☐
- **e** Mowgli goes to an old city. ☐
- **f** Shere Khan and Kaa fight. ☐
- **g** Mowgli meets his mother and father again. ☐

3 Answer the questions about the story.

- **a** Why does Mowgli live in the jungle – what do you think?
- **b** Is he going to leave the jungle one day? Why or why not?

Chapter One
The man cub

On a hot evening in the Seoni hills in India, some villagers ate after the **hunt**. Suddenly, they saw a **tiger**. It was Shere Khan, the man-killer with the bad leg. People ran here and there, afraid.

'My **baby**!' Messua cried. 'Where's my baby?'

'Nobody can help him now,' a villager said. 'The tiger has him.' The villagers took Messua away.

'A man cub!' Shere Khan thought. 'He can't go far. I can eat him later, after this meat.'

Just then, Father **Wolf** came. He found the baby.

'Shere Kahn is *not* going to eat him,' he thought.

---

cub a baby animal

hunt when people look for and kill animals to eat; to look for animals to kill and eat

tiger a big black, white and orange animal that eats meat

baby a very young child

wolf (*plural* **wolves**) a big grey, brown or black animal like a dog that eats meat

Father Wolf brought the baby home.
'Shall we keep him?' he asked.
'Yes. Put him with our cubs,' Mother
Wolf answered. 'Look, he isn't afraid.
I'm going to call him Mowgli.'

Later, big Shere Khan came, but he
couldn't get in. 'Give me the man
cub,' he said.
'No!' said Mother Wolf. She **showed**
him her teeth. 'He's our cub now.'
'One day, I'm going to hunt him,'
Shere Khan said angrily.
'No, he's going to hunt *you*,'
Mother Wolf answered.

One day, Father Wolf said, 'We must show our cubs
to the **wolf pack**. It's the **Law** of the **Jungle**.'

show to help someone to
see something

wolf pack a big family of wolves

law something that tells you what you
must or must not do

jungle a place with a lot of trees
and animals

That evening, the wolf pack and its friends met.
'Look at the cubs and remember them,' said Akela,
their **leader**. 'They're our **blood**.'
'A man cub!' the wolves cried when they saw Mowgli.
Just then, Shere Khan came.
'Give him to me,' the tiger said.

'Who wants the man cub in the pack?' Akela asked. 'Speak now,
or I give him to Shere Khan.'
'I want him in the pack,' said Baloo the **bear**. 'It's bad to kill a man cub.'
'Me too,' said Bagheera the **panther**. 'And I bring you meat.'
'Then he can live,' said Akela. Shere Khan walked away angrily.

leader the most important one in
a group

bear a big black, brown, white, or grey
animal with big claws

blood this is red, and you see it when
you cut your body

panther a big black or yellow-brown
animal that eats meat

3

Mowgli lived in the jungle with his wolf family. He played with his wolf brothers, and Baloo taught him the Law of the Jungle.

Bagheera and Father Wolf taught Mowgli to hunt. Soon he could move in the jungle and make no noise.

Mowgli learned the call of every animal, and how to speak with them.

Kee-ee! Good hunting, **kite**!

Sssss ... **snake** brother. We are of one blood, you and I.

kite a big red and brown bird with a white head

snake a long animal that has no legs

One day, Mowgli played with the **monkeys**, but Baloo was angry. 'You can't be friends with the monkeys,' he said. 'They eat everything, and they're bad. They don't understand the Law of the Jungle.'

One hot afternoon, Mowgli, Baloo, and Bagheera slept under the trees near some water. The monkeys watched them.

The monkeys came near to Mowgli. Then suddenly, they took him and carried him up into the trees.

monkey an animal with a long tail that climbs and lives in trees

Bagheera and Baloo heard Mowgli's cries. But the monkeys were fast, and Bagheera and Baloo were big and slow. Soon they were far behind. 'Help me!' Mowgli cried.

READING CHECK

Correct eight more mistakes in the chapter summary.

One day, some villagers were in the ~~river~~ *jungle* when Shere Khan the tiger came. Everyone ran, and Messua couldn't find her husband. Shere Khan saw the child and wanted to hunt him – after he finished the villagers' meat. But just then a panther found the boy and took him home.

Mowgli lived with a family of wolves, and he played with the other cubs. Later, Mother and Father Wolf gave Mowgli to the wolf pack. Some wolves didn't want Mowgli in the pack, but Baloo and Bagheera wanted him in the pack. Then Akela, the wolves' father, said, 'He can live.'

Baloo taught Mowgli the Road of the Jungle, and Mowgli also learned the song of every animal – from the kite to the snake. Baloo and Bagheera were friends with Mowgli and helped him, but Baloo was very happy when Mowgli played with the monkeys. Then one afternoon, the monkeys came and took Mowgli. They carried him up into the hills.

WORD WORK

1 Write words from Chapter 1 to match the things in the picture.

a ....*snake*....   **c** ....   **e** ....

b ....   **d** ....   **f** ....

2 Complete the sentences with words from Chapter 1.

a Many animals must h*unt* for their food.

b It's important to know the L _ _ of the Jungle.

c Mowgli lives with a wolf family and plays with their c _ _ _ .

d Akela is the l_ _ _ _ _ of the wolves.

e All wolves must show their young to the wolf p _ _ _ .

f 'We are of one b _ _ _ d,' Mowgli tells a snake.

GUESS WHAT

What happens in the next chapter? Tick (✔) three sentences.

a Mowgli asks Chil the kite to do something. ☐

b Mowgli lives with a monkey family. ☐

c Baloo and Bagheera talk to Kaa the snake. ☐

d Some villagers find Mowgli in the jungle. ☐

e Some animals want to kill Baloo and Bagheera. ☐

f Mowgli runs away. ☐

Chapter Two
The monkeys and the Old City

The monkeys carried Mowgli through the jungle, and **jumped** from tree to tree. Soon he was far away from Baloo and Bagheera. The trees **cut** Mowgli's arms and legs, and he could only see the sky.

Then Mowgli looked up and saw Chil the kite. 'Kee-ee!' Mowgli called to her. 'We are of one blood, kite. **Follow** the monkeys, and tell Bagheera where I am.'

At last, the monkeys arrived at the Old **City** and came down from the trees. 'You're going to live here with us, man cub,' they said.

---

jump to move suddenly from place to place

cut (*past* **cut**) to open something with a thing like a knife; a place where blood comes from your body after something hits it

follow to go after someone

city a big town

The monkeys **danced** everywhere.
'We're different to the animals in the jungle,' they told Mowgli. 'We have a city. And you're going to be our leader.'
'Then bring me bananas,' Mowgli said.
'At once!' they answered. But they soon began to fight, and forgot about the bananas.

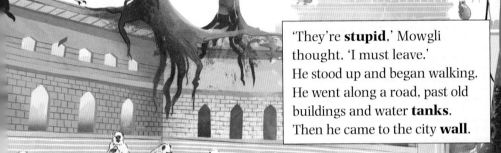

'They're **stupid**,' Mowgli thought. 'I must leave.'
He stood up and began walking.
He went along a road, past old buildings and water **tanks**.
Then he came to the city **wall**.

'You cannot leave,' the monkeys told Mowgli.
'You're our leader now.'
And they took him back.

dance to move your body and feet, for example, to music

stupid not thinking well

tank people build this to keep water in

wall something long and tall, often in a town

Chil found Baloo and Bagheera. 'Your man cub is in the Old City,' she said. 'We must help him,' Bagheera said. 'But how?' 'Let's talk to Kaa the snake,' said Baloo. 'Monkeys are afraid of him.'

'**Great** Kaa, why do the monkeys laugh at you?' Baloo asked Kaa. Kaa was very angry when he heard this.

Then Bagheera said, 'The monkeys took Mowgli. We're going to **attack** them.' 'Then I'm coming too,' said Kaa.

Bagheera and Kaa arrived at the Old City before fat, old Baloo. 'Good hunting,' said Kaa. His eyes looked cold. Then suddenly he wasn't there.

great very good, big, or important

attack to suddenly begin fighting someone

Bagheera didn't wait for Baloo. He ran into the city. When the monkeys saw him, they **threw** Mowgli from a wall down into an old building.

Soon Mowgli heard snakes in the dark. 'Ssss ... we are brothers,' he said.
'We aren't going to attack you,' the snakes answered.
'But don't stand on us!'

Bagheera **fought** well, but more and more monkeys came. 'Kill the panther!' they cried. 'Into the water!' Mowgli called, 'Monkeys can't **swim**.'
So Bagheera jumped into the water tank.

Just then, Baloo arrived. The monkeys attacked him, and Bagheera couldn't help. 'Kaa, where are you?' called Bagheera. But there was no answer.

throw (*past* **threw**) to make someone or something move through the air

fight (*past* **fought**) to hit someone again and again

swim (*past* **swam**) to go through water by moving your body

READING CHECK

Choose the correct ending for each sentence.

a Mowgli asks Chil to ...
  1 fight the monkeys.
  (2) follow the monkeys.
b The monkeys want Mowgli to ...
  1 be their leader.
  2 bring them food.
c Kaa thinks that the monkeys are ...
  1 very stupid.
  2 laughing at him.

d When Mowgli is in a dark room, he ...
  1 talks to some snakes.
  2 fights with an animal.
e After the monkeys attack Bagheera, he jumps ...
  1 over the city walls.
  2 into a water tank.
f Bagheera calls for ...
  1 Kaa.
  2 Baloo.

WORD WORK

**Read the clues and complete the words in the puzzle.
What is the mystery word in the blue squares?**

a To move your body and feet (often to music).
b A place where blood comes from your body after something hits it.
c Very important or big.
d Something long and tall, often in a town.
e A big town.
f People keep water in this building.

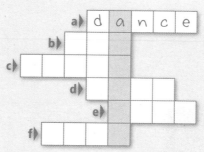

Mystery word: ....

12

ACTIVITIES

GUESS WHAT

What happens in the next chapter? Tick (✔) three pictures.

Chapter Three
Kaa's dance

Kaa heard Bagheera's call, but didn't answer. He waited quietly, then suddenly attacked. Kaa's great head hit monkeys here and there. Some died at once. The **others** ran, afraid. No monkey could fight Kaa.

Kaa went to the old building and broke down the wall. Now Mowgli was free. Then Baloo and Bagheera came. They had bad cuts.

'Go!' Kaa told them. Then he began to dance. His eyes **burned** – and when the monkeys looked into them, they couldn't run away. Slowly, they came to him. 'Let's go,' said Baloo. 'I don't want to watch Kaa when he eats!'

other(s) different; different people or animals

burn (*past* **burned**) to be on fire or to be like something on fire

That winter, the rains didn't come. Animals were thirsty. Hathi the **elephant** was leader of the jungle, and one day she spoke. 'Nobody must hunt at the river,' she said. 'All animals can drink there and be **safe**.'

So tigers, wolves, and **deer** drank at the river – and nobody was afraid.

One morning, Shere Khan came to drink. His mouth was red with blood. 'I killed a villager,' he said.
'That's bad for everybody,' the other tigers said.

'I can kill a man again ... or a man *cub*,' Shere Khan answered. He smiled at Mowgli – but he was afraid of Mowgli's eyes and couldn't look into them.

elephant a very big animal with a long nose

deer (*plural* **deer**) an animal with long legs that runs fast, and eats plants

safe in no danger

In those **dry** months, Shere Khan gave meat to the young wolves – so they began following him.

When the rains came, Shere Khan told the young wolves, 'Akela is old and can't hunt – kill him, and have a new leader. Kill Mowgli, too – he isn't your brother.'
One of Mowgli's wolf brothers, Grey Brother, was behind a **rock**. He heard Shere Khan.

dry with no water; not wet

rock a big stone

Grey Brother found Mowgli with Bagheera. 'The young wolves want to kill Akela and you,' he told them.
'What can I do?' asked Mowgli.
'Go to a village,' Bagheera answered. 'Find the red flower. Animals are afraid of it.'

Mowgli walked out of the jungle and down into a **valley**. It was dark when he arrived in a village. He **hid** and waited.

A child came past with a **fire pot**. The fire was the 'red flower', Mowgli understood now. He took it and ran away into the night.

The next night, the wolf pack met Shere Khan at the great rock. 'Akela is old and must die,' Shere Khan said.

'You can't speak here, Shere Khan!' Mowgli cried. 'You're not a wolf.' 'And are you?' Shere Khan answered.

Mowgli stood with his wolf brothers and Akela. 'Kill them all!' Shere Khan **roared**.

valley the land between two hills

hide (*past* **hid**) to go where people can't see you

fire pot people carry fire in this

roar to make a loud, deep animal noise

READING CHECK

1 Are the sentences true (T) or false (F)? Correct the false sentences with 1 or 2 words.

   Kaa

a The monkeys couldn't fight ~~Baloo~~, so they ran away. ..F..

b That winter, the rains didn't come. .....

c The animals were happy when Shere Khan came to the river after a hunt. .....

d Shere Khan couldn't look into Mowgli's eyes. .....

e Shere Khan gave some meat to the young monkeys. .....

f Some wolves wanted to kill Mowgli and Akela. .....

2 Choose the correct words to complete the sentences from the story. Then match them with the speakers in the box. Use one speaker twice.

Bagheera ~~Baloo~~ Hathi Mowgli Shere Khan

a 'I don't want to watch Kaa when he *eats / dances*'. .....Baloo.....

b 'No animals must *drink / hunt* at the river.' ....

c 'I killed a *villager / deer*.' ....

d 'Find the red *house / flower*.' ....

e 'Akela is old and must *leave / die*.' ....

f 'You can't *speak / stay* here.' ....

WORD WORK

1 Find seven more words from Chapter 3 in the word snake.

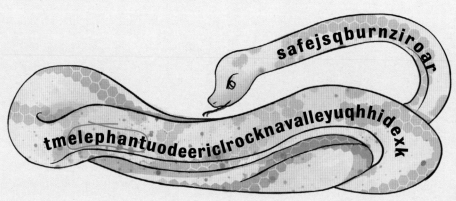

safejsqburnziroar

tmelephantuodeericlrocknavalleyuqhhidexk

ACTIVITIES

2 Match the words in Activity 1 with the definitions.

a A big animal with a long nose. ...elephant...

b To be on fire or to be like something on fire. ....

c To go in to or behind something so nobody can see you. ....

d A big stone. ....

e This brown or grey animal eats plants and runs fast. ....

f The land between two hills. ....

g To make a loud animal noise. (Tigers do this.) ....

h Not in danger. ....

GUESS WHAT

What happens in the next chapter? Tick (✔) one box to complete each sentence.

a Mowgli ...
  1 learns the language of people. ☐
  2 goes back to the old city. ☐

b Messua ...
  1 looks for Mowgli in the jungle. ☐
  2 takes Mowgli home. ☐

c One of Mowgli's wolf brothers ...
  1 tells Mowgli something important. ☐
  2 fights Shere Khan and dies. ☐

d Shere Khan ...
  1 kills Akela. ☐
  2 leaves the jungle and looks for Mowgli. ☐

Chapter Four
The village

Mowgli put a **stick** into the fire pot, and the stick began burning. The wolves attacked Akela, Mowgli, and his wolf brothers, but Mowgli burned their **fur** with the stick. They stopped, afraid of the 'red flower'.

Then Mowgli ran to Shere Khan and burned his fur with the stick. The tiger roared **in pain**. 'Akela isn't going to die,' Mowgli cried, 'not when I'm alive!'

'I was one of you,' Mowgli told the wolf pack angrily. 'I went hunting for deer with you. But now you don't want me.'
Mowgli began crying, then he turned and walked away. His wolf brothers followed him.

stick a long piece of wood from a tree

fur the hair on an animal's body

in pain feeling bad when your body is hurt

Later the next day, Mowgli left the jungle.

'I'm a boy,' he told his wolf brothers. 'I must live with people.'

When Mowgli **reached** the village, people stopped working and looked at him.
'He's **wild**!' a man cried.
'Find Messua,' said a woman.
'She lost her baby in the jungle.'

Mowgli looked at the villagers. When Messua saw Mowgli, she began crying.
'It's my boy!' she said. 'It's really him!'
'Come to our **hut** and meet your father,' she said to Mowgli. But he didn't understand – he didn't know the language of people.

That night, Mowgli slept in a tree **outside** Messua's hut.

reach to arrive at a place

wild living or thinking like an animal, not a person

hut a small house, often of wood or stone

outside in the open; not in a building

21

Mowgli's mother and father **looked after** him. But he didn't want to be in a hut at night — he always slept outside.

Mowgli watched the villagers, and he slowly learned about people. He learned about **clothes**, money, and bread.

'This is a knife,' his father told him one day. 'It's for you.'

Mowgli played with the village children. And after a few months, he could talk to them.

look after to do things for someone and help them

clothes people wear these

One night, six months later, the villagers talked under a big tree. Mowgli listened.

'The wild boy can understand us now,' the village leader said. 'He can work.'

'He can look after the **buffalo**,' said Buldeo, the village hunter.

Every day after that, Mowgli took the buffalo out into the **fields**.

One day, Grey Brother came. 'You really look like a man now,' he laughed, 'But your brothers are wolves, remember.'

Then Grey Brother stopped laughing. 'Shere Khan left the jungle yesterday,' he said. 'Chil the Kite saw him. He's coming here. He wants to kill you.'

buffalo (*plural* **buffalo**) a big animal like a cow

field a piece of land for a farmer

ACTIVITIES

READING CHECK

1 Put these sentences about Mowgli in the correct order. Number them 1–7.

Mowgli ...

a met Messua and his father. ☐

b spoke to Grey Brother near the village. ☐

c learned the language of people. ☐

d started to cry. ☐

e burned Shere Khan's fur. ☐1

f looked after the buffalo in the fields. ☐

g left the jungle. ☐

2 Complete the sentences with a name or 1 or 2 words.

a Mowgli put a .....*stick*..... into the fire pot.

b The wolves were afraid of the ....

c Mowgli walked away from the wolf pack, and his .... followed him.

d One of the villagers said, 'Find ....!' when she saw Mowgli.

e Mowgli didn't want to sleep in a ....

f .... was the village hunter.

g Mowgli took the .... out into the fields.

WORD WORK

1 Write words from Chapter 4 to match the pictures.

a c _ _ _ _ _ _

b b _ _ _ _ _ _

24

c s _ _ _ _

d f _ _

e h _ _

f f _ _ _ _ _

2 Complete the sentences with the words from Activity 1.

a It began to rain. Soon Buldeo's ...clothes... were wet.

b The villagers worked in the .... all day under the hot sun.

c .... are big animals, and they can be very dangerous.

d Mowgli put a .... into the fire and it began to burn.

e Messua and her husband lived in a village ....

f Tigers have got orange, black, and white ....

GUESS WHAT

What happens in the next chapter? Write *Yes* or *No*.

a The villagers build a hut for Mowgli. ....

b Mowgli's wolf brothers help him to fight Shere Khan. ....

c Buldeo hunts Shere Khan. ....

d The villagers want to kill Messua and her husband. ....

e There is a lot of rain, and the villagers lose their huts. ....

f Bagheera comes to the village. ....

g Mowgli sits on an elephant. ....

Chapter Five
Wolf boy

The next morning, Mowgli saw his wolf brothers in the fields. Then Akela **appeared**. Mowgli put his arms **around** him. 'Shere Khan is in a **ravine** near the village,' Akela said. 'He's going to attack you tonight, when you bring the buffalo home.'
'I **need** your help,' Mowgli said.

That evening, Mowgli took the buffalo down the road to the village. When they reached the ravine, the wolves appeared. The buffalo were afraid and ran into the ravine.

'Come out and fight, Shere Khan!' cried Mowgli.
The tiger roared and came along the ravine. Then he saw the buffalo ... and ran.

appear to be suddenly in front of someone's eyes

around all the way round something

ravine a small valley

need when something is important to have

Shere Khan couldn't get out of the ravine, or run faster than the buffalo. Soon they reached him. With a great roar, Shere Khan died.

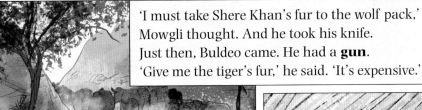

'I must take Shere Khan's fur to the wolf pack,' Mowgli thought. And he took his knife.
Just then, Buldeo came. He had a **gun**.
'Give me the tiger's fur,' he said. 'It's expensive.'

Suddenly, the wolves appeared.
Akela jumped on Buldeo.
Mowgli spoke in wolf calls.
'Don't kill him,' he told Akela.

Later, Buldeo ran to the village. 'That boy can speak with wolves,' he said. 'He isn't really a person – he's a wolf-boy!'

gun people fight with this

Mowgli carried the fur of Shere Khan to the jungle. He left it on the big rock, then he called Baloo, Bagheera, and the wolf pack.
'I killed Shere Khan,' he said. 'Now you are free.'
'Be our leader,' cried the wolves.
'No,' answered Mowgli, and he walked away.

'I must leave,' Mowgli told Mother and Father Wolf.
'We're coming with you,' his wolf brothers said.
'No,' Mowgli answered. 'I'm going to the man pack. You must stay in the jungle.'

evil very bad

But when Mowgli reached the village, people cried, 'Go away, **evil** wolf!' They attacked him with sticks and rocks.

Mowgli was **worried** about Messua and his father, so that night he quietly went back to the village.

Some villagers were under the big tree. 'We must kill the wolf-boy's mother and father,' Buldeo told them. 'They're wolf-people, too. They're evil!'

Mowgli went to Messua's hut. 'Mother, Father ...' Mowgli called. 'The villagers are going to kill you! You must leave now!'

'How can we run away?' asked his father. 'Some of the villagers have horses. They can easily **catch** us.' 'And we can't go through the jungle at night,' Messua said. 'Wild animals can hunt us there.'

worried not happy about something and thinking about it a lot

catch (*past* **caught**) to take or stop someone or something quickly

ACTIVITIES

READING CHECK

1 Match the words with the characters who say them.

a Go away, evil wolf. ☐

b Give me the tiger's fur. It's expensive. ☐

c Don't kill him. ☐

d Now you are free. ☐

e We can't go through the jungle at night. ☐

f Come out and fight, Shere Khan. ☐

g He isn't really a person. ☐

1 **Mowgli** says this when the buffalo run into the ravine.

2 **Buldeo** says this to Mowgli when he sees Shere Khan's body.

3 **Mowgli** says this to Akela when the wolf attacks Buldeo.

4 **Buldeo** says this when he tells the villagers about Mowgli.

5 **Mowgli** says this to the wolf pack after he brings them the fur of Shere Khan.

6 **The villagers** say this when they see Mowgli again.

7 **Messua** says this when Mowgli wants his mother and father to leave the village.

2 Are the sentences true (T) or false (F)?

a Shere Khan died because he couldn't get out of the ravine. ..T..

b Buldeo helped Mowgli to hunt Shere Khan. .....

c The villagers were happy when they saw Mowgli again. .....

d The wolf pack wanted Mowgli to be their leader. .....

e After he heard the villagers, Mowgli went to Messua's hut. .....

f Messua and her husband left the village on a horse. .....

WORD WORK

1 Unscramble the words from Chapter 5.

a ......evil...... **d** ....

b .... **e** ....

c .... **f** ....

a liev   **d** nug

b inevar   **e** tacch

c reidrow   **f** aearpp

30

2 Use the words in Activity 1 to complete the sentences.

a That boy is very bad – he's ......*evil*..... .

b As the buffalo went down the ravine, the wolves began to ....

c Shere Khan ran along the ...., away from the buffalo.

d Buldeo used his .... to hunt in the jungle.

e Mowgli was very .... about his mother and father.

f 'The villagers on horses can easily .... us,' said Messua.

GUESS WHAT

What happens in the next chapter? Tick (✔) an ending to complete each sentence.

a The villagers ...

1 catch Messua and Mowgli's father.

2 run from Bagheera.

b Messua ...

1 has a baby.

2 is very ill and dies.

c A pack of red dogs ...

1 attack the village.

2 fight with the wolf pack.

d Mowgli ...

1 stays in the jungle with his wolf brothers.

2 goes to live in a village.

Chapter Six
Mowgli leaves the jungle

Just then, Bagheera came. 'The villagers attacked you, Mowgli,' he said. 'Chil the Kite told us. Your wolf brothers are waiting for you outside the village.'

'Go now,' Bagheera told Mowgli. 'But I'm going to wait here.'

Later, some angry villagers came to the hut. They opened the door and saw Bagheera. 'Run!' they cried.

Bagheera walked around the village and roared, so nobody left their hut all night!

'I must leave you,' Mowgli told his mother and father on the road. 'You're safe in the jungle because my wolf brothers are following you. Don't be afraid of them.'

The next day ...

Mowgli was with Akela when Chil came.
'Your mother and father are safe, Mowgli,' she said. 'But I've got bad **news**. A pack of red dogs came into the jungle this morning.'

Akela was worried. 'Red dogs have no Law of the Jungle,' he said. 'They kill everything ... deer, wolves, monkeys ...'
'We must fight them,' cried Mowgli.

news when someone tells you something new

'But Mowgli, perhaps the wolf pack is going to die,' Akela said. 'And you aren't a wolf. The pack didn't want you ... remember. Leave now!'
'No,' answered Mowgli. 'I'm still a wolf. But we need more help to fight the red dogs.'

'Great Kaa,' Mowgli asked later. 'How can the wolf pack fight the red dogs?' 'There's a good **place** near the river,' Kaa answered. 'The **bees** live there. It's the best place to fight the dogs.'

The next day ...

Mowgli was in a tree near the river when the red dogs came. 'Hey, stupid dogs!' he cried. 'We're going to kill you,' called the dogs' leader. 'Then catch me,' cried Mowgli, and he jumped from tree to tree.

'Come on, fat dogs!' Mowgli called. 'Are you afraid?'

place where something is

bee a small animal with wings that makes honey

Mowgli ran across the rocks. He hit the trees with a stick, and the bees came out.

Mowgli jumped from a **cliff** into the river and swam to Kaa. Behind him, the bees attacked the red dogs.

The dogs cried in pain and jumped into the water. The fast river carried many away. The others swam across the river – to the wolves. The wolf pack fought the dog pack, and many dogs and wolves died. In the end, the red dogs ran away.

Akela was nearly dead when Mowgli found him after the fight. 'I **saved** you once, Mowgli,' Akela said, 'and today you saved the pack. But you must go back to your people one day. It's in your blood.' Then Akela died.

cliff a natural wall of rock

save to stop bad things happening to someone

When Mowgli was seventeen, his wolf mother and father died. Mowgli was very **sad**. That spring, Mowgli began thinking about Messua. He wanted to see her – and people – again.

One day, Mowgli left the jungle and walked all day. It was evening when he saw a village with a great, old building. He went into the village and hid.

Mowgli watched the villagers. Then, in a window, he saw a woman with a baby. It was Messua!

sad not happy

'Mowgli, my son,' she cried when he appeared. She put her arms around him. 'This is your brother,' his father said.

The next day, Mowgli went back to the jungle and spoke to his wolf brothers. 'Akela was right,' he told them. 'I must go back to my people. I have a man-brother now.'

Later, Mowgli said goodbye to Bagheera, Baloo, and Kaa. 'We're old now,' Baloo said sadly. 'But you're still young. Come and see us.'

Mowgli left the jungle with his wolf brothers. 'Goodbye,' he said to them when they saw the village. 'You must go back now, before any people see you.' 'Come and hunt with us sometimes,' Grey Brother said. 'We are of one blood.'

READING CHECK

1 Put the sentences in the correct order. Number them 1–8.

a The wolves and the red dogs fought. ☐

b Mowgli went to live with people. ☐

c Messua met Mowgli again. ☐

d Mowgli sat in a tree and called to the red dogs. ☐

e Chil told Mowgli and Akela some bad news. ☐

f Mowgli's mother and father left their village. ☐

g Mowgli jumped from a cliff into the river. ☐

h Mother and Father Wolf died. ☐

2 Correct the sentences. Use a name or 1 or 2 words.

a Some angry villagers ran when they saw ~~Baloo~~. *Bagheera*

b Akela wanted Mowgli to stay before the red dogs came.

c Kaa told Mowgli about a place near the village – a good place to fight.

d Many wolves and snakes died in a big fight.

e Mowgli spoke to Grey Brother before the old wolf died.

f When he was seventeen, Mowgli left the jungle and went to a field.

g Mowgli lived with his mother, father, and baby sister, but he also visited his wolf brothers sometimes.

WORD WORK

1 Read the clues and complete the crossword with words from Chapter 6.

Down

1 A natural wall of rock.

2 These small animals with wings make honey.

4 When someone tells you something new.

Across

3 Where something is.

5 To stop bad things happening to someone.

6 Not happy.

38

2 Use the correct form of the words from Activity 1 to complete the sentences.

a They couldn't get out of the ravine because there were high ..cliffs.. all around them.

b I've got some great .... – Mowgli has come home!

c We must .... animals from hunters like Buldeo.

d Mowgli felt very .... when Akela died.

e .... are very small animals, but they can attack you if they're angry.

f Mowgli knows a great .... to swim in the river.

WHAT NEXT?

1 What happens after the story ends? Tick (✔) some of these ideas. Then write two ideas of your own.

a Mowgli often visits Kaa, Baloo, and Bagheera. ☐

b Mowgli is unhappy in the village and goes back to the wolf pack. ☐

c Messua and her family meet Mowgli's wolf brothers. ☐

d The monkeys leave the Old City when people come there. ☐

e Buldeo comes to a new village and tells people about the 'wolf-boy'. ☐

f Mowgli loves a young woman. They live in a house near the jungle. ☐

g ....

h ....

2 What happens to these characters after the story ends? Write sentences with ideas of your own.

| Buldeo   Mowgli's younger brother   Kaa the snake |

Project A *Writing a performing monologue*

1 **Read these new lines for the story. Who said them? Complete the descriptions a–f with the characters' names.**

 Baloo   **Buldeo**   **Kaa**   **Messua**   **Mowgli**   **Shere Khan**

> Don't take me away! I must go back and find my baby.

> He's very good with animals. He can work for us and look after the buffalo.

a .... says this to the other villagers in the jungle.

b .... says this to the villagers one night.

> Why do you want him in the pack, stupid wolves? I can't fight you all now, but I'm going to eat him one day.

> Jump from the cliff into the river. I'm going to wait for you there.

c .... says this to the wolf pack.

d .... says this to Mowgli.

> Bagheera and I couldn't follow the monkeys – they're very fast.

> Don't worry. I'm not going to forget you.

e .... says this to Kaa the snake.

f .... says this to Kaa, Baloo, and Bagheera.

2 A 'monologue' is a long speech by a character in a story or play. Complete these monologues with the words in the boxes.

| build | fight | forget | leader | live | stupid | understand |

I don't want to **a)** .... with you – or be your
b) .... You think that you're better than the other animals,
but you're **c)** .... , and you don't **d)** .... the Law
of the Jungle. You **e)** .... all the time and **f)** ....
things, too. You talk about 'our city', but you didn't **g)** ....
this place – and you don't know what all these buildings are.

Mowgli

| attacked | evil | gun | hunt | ravine | village | wolf |

I was down in the **h)** .... when I saw that boy – the wild boy. He was
next to a dead tiger. I think that it was Shere Khan, the man-killer. When he saw
me, he suddenly changed into a **i)** .... and he **j)** ....
me. I lost my **k)** .... and I nearly died. I tell you, that boy is
l) .... He isn't a man – he's a wolf. We must **m)** ....
him before he comes to our **n)** .... and kills one of us.

Buldeo

3 Write another monologue. Use the notes for A or B.

A

The villagers attack Mowgli with sticks and rocks. Mowgli goes back to the village and talks to them. Mowgli says:
- he lived with them, learned their language, and looked after their animals.
- they called him 'evil' and threw stones.
- he understands now: he's a wolf.
- he's going to live in the jungle.

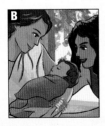
B

Messua meets Mowgli again when he is seventeen. She says:
- she always thought of him.
- she has a baby now – Mowgli's brother.
- she wants Mowgli to live with them.
- he can visit the jungle.

41

Project B *Jungle animals*

1 Read about the Indian python and answer the questions.

   a How long do Indian pythons live?

   b How big are they when they are born, and when they are adults?

   c Where do they hunt, and what do they eat?

   d Why are they in danger?

The Indian python

The Indian python lives in India and southern Asia – from Pakistan in the west to Sri Lanka in the east. It's usually white, black, and brown in colour. Indian pythons live for about 34 years, and Kaa in *The Jungle Book* is an old python.

Baby pythons are born from eggs – about 100 babies at one time.

The pythons are about 45 cm long when they come out of their eggs, but **adult** Indian pythons can be 6 m long and **weigh** 90 kg!

Pythons live and find their food near rivers. They only eat meat, but they hunt a lot of different animals, like deer, small cats, and monkeys. After pythons eat a big animal, they don't move much for a long time – sometimes months!

Today, Indian pythons are **in danger** because people are hunting them – or burning the jungle to make farms or houses.

adult old and not a child

weigh how big somebody or something is

in danger when you can die

2 Read the factfile and complete the text about the Asian elephant.

Factfile Asian elephant

Where?	In jungles in south-east Asia, from India and Nepal to Borneo
How big?	About 1 m when born. Adults usually 2.4–2.75 m and 2,400–2,700 kg.
Lives?	50–60 years (**Females** and young live in groups called herds. **Males** live alone.)
Eats?	**Plants** and small trees (150 kg a day)
In danger?	Yes (Their jungles are smaller every year, and people hunt them.)

The Asian elephant

Asian elephants are the biggest land animals in Asia, and the second biggest in the world (after the African elephant). They can live for about 60 years.

Most elephants are about 1 m tall when they are small, but **a)** .... elephants are between 2.4 and 2.75 m tall – and weigh up to **b)** .... kg!

Asian elephants live in **c)** .... in south-east Asia, and they eat **d)** .... and small trees. They have to eat a lot of them, too – about **e)** .... every day!

Male Asian elephants live **f)** .... , but females and their children live in groups called **g)** .... The leaders of the group are usually old females, and the elephants follow the **rules** of their herd: a little like the 'Law of the Jungle'.

Sadly, Asian elephants are in danger today. Hunters kill them, and jungles in Asia are now much smaller than in the past.

female girls and women

male boys and men

plant something like a flower or tree

rule something you must do

3 Choose one of these animals and find information about it online. Then write notes. Use the headings in the factfile in Activity 2 to help you.

The Bengal tiger

The wolf

The black panther

The brown bear

4 Write a profile of the animal that you chose in Activity 3.

- Use your notes in Activity 3 to help you.
- Find photos on the internet.
- Print out your profile to display, or prepare a presentation for your class.

GRAMMAR

GRAMMAR CHECK

can / can't and *could / couldn't*

We use can + infinitive without *to* to talk about things that are possible, or that we are able to do. *They can attack you if they are angry.*   *Then Mowgli can live.*

We use can't + infinitive without *to* to talk about things that aren't possible, or that we aren't able to do. *You can't be friends with the monkeys.*

We use could or couldn't + infinitive without *to* to talk about things that we were or weren't able to do in the past.

Soon Mowgli could move in the jungle and make no noise.   *Big Shere Khan couldn't go in.*

1 Choose the correct words to complete the text.

The villagers stopped eating their food. They **a)** *can / could* hear an animal in the jungle,

but what was it? Suddenly a tiger came out of the trees. The villagers **b)** *can't / couldn't* kill

a tiger, so they ran, afraid.

'I **c)** *can't / can* find my baby!' cried Messua.

'Come with us,' one of the men said. 'You **d)** *can / can't* save your baby now – the tiger has it.'

The man **e)** *can / could* see the baby, but he **f)** *couldn't / could* reach him because of the tiger.

The villagers took Messua away, and she **g)** *could / couldn't* do anything.

Shere Khan began to eat the villagers' meat. Then he saw the baby. 'I **h)** *can / couldn't* eat him

later,' he thought, 'but first I **i)** *could / can* finish this meat. The man cub **j)** *could / can't* go far.'

2 Complete the sentences with *can, can't, could*, or *couldn't*.

a 'I ...... can ..... speak to all the animals,' Mowgli said happily.

b Everyone was afraid of Kaa because nobody .... fight him.

c The monkeys don't go into the water tanks because they .... swim.

d 'We were very worried about you,' Baloo said. 'We .... find you.'

e 'Akela is old,' Shere Khan told the young wolves. 'He .... be the leader of

your pack any more.'

f When Mowgli first went to the village, he .... speak the language of people.

g Bagheera .... see a deer near the river, so he moved very quietly through

the trees.

h 'You .... come to the jungle and visit us any time,' Grey Brother told Mowgli.

45

GRAMMAR CHECK

Plural nouns

We add -s to nouns to make them plural.

village   villages

When a noun ends in -o or -ch, we usually add -es.

watch   watches

When a noun ends in a consonant + y, we change the y to i and add -es.

family   families

When a noun ends in -fe, it usually changes to -ves.

knife   knives

Some nouns have irregular plurals.

deer   deer   person   people

3 **Write the plurals of these nouns. Use a dictionary to help you.**

a foot .....feet.....

b country ....

c sandwich ....

d city ....

e wife ....

f monkey ....

g buffalo ....

h sheep ....

i story ....

j man ....

4 **Write the plural words under the pictures.**

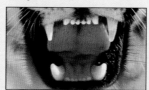

a c hildren.....

b t................

c w................

d s................

e d................

f b................

GRAMMAR CHECK

Adjectives and adverbs of manner

We use adjectives to describe things and people.

One hot afternoon, Mowgli, Baloo, and tired Bagheera slept under the trees.

We use adverbs to talk about how we do something.

Kaa waited quietly, then suddenly attacked.

To make adverbs from adjectives, we usually add -ly.   *quiet   quietly*
For adjectives that end in a consonant and -y, we change -y to -ily.   *angry   angrily*

One day I'm going to hunt him, Shere Khan said angrily.

Some adverbs are irregular. You must learn these forms.

The man cub can't go far.   Bagheera fought well, but more and more monkeys came.

5 **Look at the word lists below. Choose the correct word to complete the text.**

a 1 easy	2 great	3 (happily)		**e** 1 angrily	2 angry	3 unhappily
b 1 well	2 good	3 carefully		**f** 1 carefully	2 good	3 careful
c 1 quiet	2 quietly	3 noisily		**g** 1 badly	2 noisily	3 bad
d 1 well	2 good	3 easy				

Mowgli lived **a)** ...happily... in the jungle with his wolf family, and Baloo taught him

the Law of the Jungle. Mowgli was a **b)** .... learner. He learned how to move

c) .... in the jungle – because you can't hunt **d)** .... when animals

can hear you.

One day, Baloo was very **e)** .... with him.

'Listen very **f)** ....,' Baloo told Mowgli. 'Never play with the monkeys. They're stupid,

g) .... animals, and they don't understand the Law of the Jungle.'

6 **Look at the sentences below. Some are wrong. Change the form of the adjective or adverb to correct them. Tick (✔) the sentences that are correct.**

a It was very ~~darkly~~ in the jungle, and the villagers were afraid.   .....dark.....

b Baloo was an old, fat bear. He moved very slow.   ....

c 'I'm tired,' said Mowgli. And he sat down by the river.   ....

d The monkeys could jump from tree to tree very easy.   ....

e The red dogs aren't nicely animals. They kill everything.   ....

f Mowgli was very sad when Mother and Father Wolf died.   ....

g 'My beautifully boy!' Messua said when she saw Mowgli.   ....

GRAMMAR

GRAMMAR CHECK

Prepositions of movement

Prepositions of movement tell us where something moves to.

Mowgli put a stick into the fire pot.   *Shere Khan ran along the ravine.*

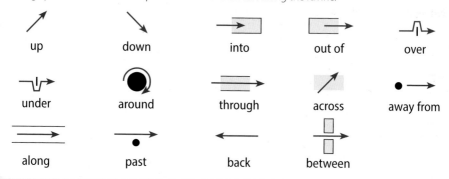

up   down   into   out of   over

under   around   through   across   away from

along   past   back   between

7 Choose the correct words to complete the text.

The monkeys took Mowgli **a)** *up* / *in* a tree and carried him **b)** *into* / *away* from his friends. Baloo and Bagheera couldn't follow the monkeys **c)** *along* / *through* the jungle for long, and soon they were far behind.

The monkeys jumped from tree to tree. They carried Mowgli **d)** *under* / *over* the hills, **e)** *across* / *between* the river, and **f)** *into* / *under* the Old City. Then they came **g)** *up* / *down* from the trees and left Mowgli on a stone building. Mowgli sat and watched the monkeys. They ran here and there, and danced **h)** *around* / *up* him.

'They're stupid,' Mowgli thought. 'I must leave this place.' He stood up and began walking. He went **i)** *into* / *along* a road, **j)** *past* / *back* old buildings and water tanks. Then he came to the city walls. He wanted to go **k)** *out of* / *through* the city, but the monkeys stopped him.

'You cannot leave,' they told him. 'You're our leader now.'

GRAMMAR

GRAMMAR CHECK

Past Simple: affirmative and negative

To make the Past Simple affirmative of regular verbs, we usually add -d or -ed to the infinitive without *to*. *At last, the monkeys arrived at the Old City.*

With verbs that end in a consonant + -y, we change -y to -i and add -ed.

worry – Mowgli was worried.

Some verbs are irregular. You must learn their Past Simple forms.

have   had   run   ran   go   went   say   said

To make the Past Simple negative, we use *didn't* (*did not*) + infinitive without *to*.

lived – Mowgli didn't live in the village.   went – He didn't go to school.

The verb be has an irregular negative form.

was   were   wasn't   weren't

8   Complete the text with the correct form of the verbs in brackets.

When Messua **a)** ......*saw*...... (see) Mowgli, she **b)** .... (begin) crying.

'It's my boy!' she **c)** .... (tell) the villagers. 'It's really him.'

She **d)** .... (put) her arms around Mowgli and **e)** .... (say),

'Come to our hut.' But Mowgli **f)** .... (not understand) her because he

g) .... (not know) the language of people.

Mowgli's mother and father **h)** .... (be) very happy, and they **i)** .... (give)

him something to eat. He **j)** .... (feel) safe with them, but he

k) .... (not want) to be in a hut that night – he **l)** .... (sleep) outside.

9   Complete the sentences with the affirmative or negative form of the verbs in brackets. Use the verbs in any order.

a   Bagheera ...*waited*... for Baloo. He .... into the Old City. (wait / run)

b   Kaa .... Bagheera's call but .... (hear / not answer)

c   That winter, the rains .... The animals .... thirsty. (be / come)

d   Akela .... on Buldeo, but he .... the old hunter. (jump / not kill)

e   Mowgli often .... a knife, but he .... it to hunt. (need / carry)

f   Mowgli .... behind a wall, so the villagers .... him. (hide / not see)

g   When Mowgli .... the jungle, he .... his wolf brothers.
(not forget / leave)

49

GRAMMAR

GRAMMAR CHECK

Going to **future: affirmative, negative, and questions**

We use *going to* to talk about plans, intentions, and to make predictions.

We make the *going to* future with the correct form of the verb be + going to + the infinitive without *to.*

Affirmative – *I'm going to call him Mowgli. (= plan)*

Negative – *Akela isn't going to die. Not when I'm alive! (= prediction)*

Question – *Are you going to be our leader? (= intention)*

10 Complete the dialogue with *going to* and the correct form of the words in brackets.

Messua: What **a)** are we going to do (we / do)? The villagers
b) .... (kill) us.

Mowgli: I **c)** .... (I / help) you, but you must leave now.

Father: How **d)** .... (Messua and I / run) away, Mowgli? The villagers have got horses and we must walk. We **e)** .... (not reach) the next village before they catch us.

Mowgli: Don't worry – people **f)** .... (not follow) you. I can stay here and stop them.

Messua: But we must go through the jungle, and there are wild animals there.
g) .... (they / hunt) us?

Mowgli: You **h)** .... (be) safe in the jungle. The animals **i)** ....
(not attack) because my wolf brothers **j)** .... (follow) you.

11 Complete the sentences with *going to* and the words in the box.

be	~~come~~ fight hide leave stay wait

a There isn't much water in the river now. When are the rains . going to come . again?

b One day soon, Akela .... the leader of the pack any more.

c Shere Khan .... for Mowgli in the ravine.

d How are we .... the red dogs, Kaa?

e The villagers .... in their homes tonight because Bagheera is outside.

f Mowgli 's mother and father .... in the jungle so the angry village people can't see them.

g Is Mowgli .... the jungle?

GRAMMAR CHECK

Information questions and Yes/No questions

We use question words, for example *Who* or *How*, in information questions, and we answer them by giving information. The question word comes before the auxiliary verb.

'How can we run away?' his father asked.

'Great Kaa,' Baloo said, 'why do the monkeys laugh at you?'

When the question is about the subject of a sentence, we don't need an auxiliary verb.

'Who wants the man cub in the pack?' Akela asked.

Yes/No questions start with the verb or auxiliary verb.

Can Mowgli talk to the animals?   Yes, he can.

12 Complete the questions with the words in the box. Then tick (✔) the information questions.

| Are   Can   How   What   When   Where   Who   ~~Why~~ |

a   ......Why...... did Shere Khan want the man cub?   ✔

b   .... monkeys swim?   ☐

c   .... did Baloo and Bagheera know Mowgli was in the Old City?   ☐

d   .... did Mowgli use to burn Shere Khan's fur?   ☐

e   .... is the leader of the jungle?   ☐

f   .... there many other tigers in the jungle?   ☐

g   .... do the bees live?   ☐

h   .... did Mowgli leave the jungle?   ☐

13 Match the answers with the questions in Activity 12.

1 In some trees next to a cliff and the river.   ☐

2 Hathi the elephant.   ☐

3 Because Chil told them where he was.   ☐

4 No, they can't – and they don't like the water.   ☐

5 He left when he was seventeen.   ☐

6 Yes, there are. And they don't like Shere Khan.   ☑

7 Because the tiger wanted to eat him.   ☐

8 He used a burning stick.   ☐

DOMINOES Your Choice

Read *Dominoes* for pleasure, or to develop language skills. It's your choice.

Each *Dominoes* reader includes:
- a good story to enjoy
- integrated activities to develop reading skills and increase vocabulary
- task-based projects – perfect for CEFR portfolios
- contextualized grammar activities.

Each *Dominoes* pack contains a reader and an excitingly dramatized audio recording of the story.

If you liked this *Domino*, read these:

Jemma's Jungle Adventure
Anne Collins

Jemma is very excited when she joins an expedition to the island of Kamora. She hopes to learn about doing scientific research, and to find a very rare bird of paradise.

She is happy to meet the famous Dr Malone and the wise Dr Al Barwani, and to help to research birds, snakes, and insects. But things start to go wrong. Someone has a terrible secret, and there is danger for Jemma – and for the bird.

Who has a secret plan, and what is it? What will happen to the bird? And what will happen to Jemma?

Who am I?
Or, the Modern Frankenstein
Emma Howell

Vic has no friends. Everyone else has friends, and it makes him angry. So, Vic makes a new name for himself online, so he can make other people feel the way he does. But soon Vic finds it difficult to control what he has created …

Will Vic's mistake hurt people, or can he stop it in time? What will happen to Vic? And what will happen to the monster he has made?

	CEFR	Cambridge Exams	IELTS	TOEFL iBT	TOEIC
Level 3	B1	PET	4.0	57-86	550
Level 2	A2–B1	KET-PET	3.0-4.0	–	390
Level 1	A1–A2	YLE Flyers/KET	3.0	–	225
Starter & Quick Starter	A1	YLE Movers	1.0–2.0	–	–

You can find details and a full list of books and teachers' resources on our website:
www.oup.com/elt/gradedreaders